The Unsheltered HEART

"Put not your trust in princes," the prophets say. Father Raab urges love of the poor and the afflicted through conversion of our hearts—prompted by his profoundly challenging and distinctive Advent meditations.

Nicholas Ayo, C.S.C.
Author of *Gloria Patri*

In a season when most of us are lulled into torpor by too much—food, drink, partying, shopping—Ron Raab's *The Unsheltered Heart* is a gentle but firm wake-up call to find our true selves in God by exposing our hearts to God's Word. The simple, practical format will make it not another obligation, but a welcome respite for those wishing to deepen their Advent experience.

Bernadette Gasslein
Editor of *Celebrate!: The Pastoral Magazine with the Liturgical Heart*

Cycle B

The Unsheltered HEART

an at-home advent retreat

Ronald Patrick Raab, c.s.c.

ave maria press AmP notre dame, indiana

Founded in 1865, Ave Maria Press is a ministry of the United States Province of Holy Cross.

www.avemariapress.com

ISBN-10 1-59471-284-0 ISBN-13 978-1-59471-284-5

Cover image © Malaika Favorite.

Cover and text design by Brian C. Conley.

Printed and bound in the United States of America.

green press INITIATIVE

In gratitude for all on the margins of society,
who teach me to believe in God's love.

Contents

Preface

During the Advent season I grow more conscious of people who feel they do not belong in the world. My entire being feels the deep sadness and anger of an elderly woman staring at me from our sidewalk as she piles her wet belongings into a shopping cart and pulls her stocking cap over her ears. In our chapel confessional, I hear the heartbreaking words of emotional and sexual promiscuity among so many married people. The hearts of many people are divided because of loneliness, fear, and painful histories of personal conflict and violence. So many people ache to belong in healthy human relationships and ultimately in a relationship with God. I struggle to shore up my own prayer life as I hear the stories of utter loneliness because so many people cannot let go of the past.

These four weeks of preparation for the celebration of the Incarnation wring mostly tears of abandonment from the hearts of those who live in poverty. For many, family ties were cut decades ago because of addictions or generational abuse or long-term mental illness. Many hard-working people feel unwelcomed in society because of their lack of formal education. Some people have lost love and intimacy in their marriages, while others have never once found the love they truly desire. Some people feel they just do not fit in, while others refer to themselves as the "black sheep" of their families. So many people live dissatisfied lives no matter how much money they earn or what status they have in society. Some feel lost because of past decisions, and others feel wrongly judged for whom they love in the present.

I minister among people who courageously face the cold winters living outside. Some people living with mental illness feel they do not belong in society because Christmas—as advertised—belongs to people with physical beauty, bountiful wealth, and stable emotional intimacy. Some of our neighbors simply hide deep within bottles of booze or shoot heroin and wait for the holiday season to subside. These people feel most at home in denial and numbness. Endless hangovers and shaky withdrawals enable people to at least feel something.

These stories break my heart during the Advent season. The circumstances of our elderly poor or the teenage streetwalkers looking for a hookup wear me down. I have choices in these Advent days: I can look the other way as I approach a shoeless man pushing his shopping cart in the pouring rain, or I can look at him and begin to really see the struggle of his life. Through my years of ministry here in Portland, I have learned that I must make the choice to look at the poverty around me and so unshelter my heart, my imagination, my generosity, and my ability to offer solace.

I also must not be deaf to the ancient scriptural prophets who still pierce the winter's cold. These familiar voices offer a wake-up call for all people to believe again in God. If I am deaf to God's revelation in the scriptures, then I remain deaf and unforgiving to the people who come to me exhausted from the pressures of life. God calls us to realize a deep sense of belonging if we enter into the mystery that Jesus took on flesh. Suffering people are no less human than Jesus. We must open up our human hearts to break apart our bigotry, neglect, and phobias. If we continue to celebrate Christ Jesus in our midst, then our hearts must become unsheltered from the judgments that separate us from other people.

Introduction

As Advent dawns again this year, I muster the courage to believe that people's emptiness and long-time searching are also the places in which God longs to be born. I cannot force people to feel loved by God, and I cannot convince people that strangers care about them. Yet I can offer people the experiences of hope that Christ has planted within me.

The real miracle of this season is that people who are powerless in society offer me love and teach me to remain open to life. Love abides in people who live unsheltered lives in cold weather and in the emotional storms of bitterness and indifference. When I am in genuine and honest relationships with people who live with so much less, I am open to a new abundance that I often ignore in my own life. In the Advent season I realize that I belong in the creation of God, among all people who hunger and thirst for justice and honor.

The season of Advent leads us to the celebration of Christmas, the miracle of God-made-flesh. This reality of God's love among us blurs the boundaries of heaven and earth. Divine love still lives under our skin. Jesus is here regardless of how alienated we feel from one another. This season of Advent opens us to God's plan—that every person is welcomed and loved in every corner of the earth. This spiritual reality so often is diminished in our desire to put boundaries and limits on who is eligible for God's forgiveness and mercy. Living our lives in the freedom of an open and generous spirit, we experience love coming alive again in all of our relationships. God-among-us is the love we all seek with an unsheltered heart in this season of patient waiting and profound longing.

The Structure of This Retreat

Each week of this at-home retreat follows the same simple format. You are asked to read the Sunday gospel text not just on Sunday, but every day in order to stay focused and experience a deepening appreciation of its message to you. You will be prompted each day to respond in writing to the text: reflection upon your own life and your encounter with God. Each day's retreat time ends with a prayer of your own creation, whether written or simply formed in the silence of your heart. This retreat unfolds in the following five steps.

Step 1. Welcome the Stranger Called Silence

December seldom provides time for personal silence. For most people, reflection time evaporates into preparing for family gatherings, making lists, shopping, attending required business parties, visiting with friends, and connecting with loved ones far away. Silence in this season often seems an unwelcome stranger.

I invite you to make sufficient time for silent prayer and reflection during these holy days of Advent. You will hear the gospel readings during Sunday Eucharist; but decision-making and planning are essential if you hope to set aside time to allow the readings to sink into your life patterns. The only way to hear the gospels and welcome the meaning of Advent and Christmas is to prepare a space in your life for silence. Prayer is a personal responsibility. My reflections here do not substitute for your prayer and silence.

Begin taking responsibility for your prayer by preparing a comfortable space where you can go to rest, pray, and reflect every day. Allow this setting to become your retreat place where you can offer God your private thoughts and authentic personal story, no matter what shape the story has taken. The messages of Advent will come alive in the quiet minutes you spend in this retreat place.

Step 2. Discover Your Story Within the Word

This retreat begins with the gospel readings from Sunday Mass. The simple lines of scripture embody the message of Christ for each person living today. Read, reflect, and ponder the passage every day during the week. Inspiration, grace, and love will flow through you when you take time to sit with God and the sacred text. Allow the events of your life to commune with God. Bring your lived story—the past and present—to the holy Word written centuries ago. You will find the echoes of God's voice rising up within your concerns, frustrations, and loneliness, as well as in your joy. Open yourself to change within God's consolation and forgiveness. Unshelter your heart and let it rest in the presence of these gospel passages.

Step 3. Connect to the Waiting World: A Weekly Theme

Each week I offer a brief thematic essay in which I share connections between the message of the gospel story and my life experience. This reflection draws out the retreat theme for the week. It may not speak to your life, work, or place in the world—I simply present these words to spark your imagination. Think about your own life and find links to the deeper story of Jesus and our faith tradition. If my reflections do not speak to you, then continue on by drawing more fully from your own experiences. This journal retreat is meant to help you relate to the gospel stories through reflection on your past and present, opening your heart to God's grace for the future.

Step 4. Respond to the Cry of the Prophets

In this section, I continue to draw connections between the gospel reading and everyday life for each day of the week. Each day brings a deeper awareness of how the message of the gospel text is to be prayed, contemplated, and lived out. These reflections and invitations are meant to get you thinking about your own life and the people who surround you on a daily basis. If the daily reflection does not resonate with your personal story, then do not pray with it, but explore your own experience to find solid ground from which to pray. Allow the rhythm of the daily reading of the scriptures to carve a path toward the coming of Christ in your own life.

For each day, I provide both questions for reflection and open-ended journaling statements to evoke more than a phrase or two from your life. I present these fill-in-the-blank sentences to prompt you to write about your thoughts, feelings, and reactions to the scriptures and your own life. These are the beginnings of your real retreat. This journal-keeping is the process where you may write honestly about your life and longing for the gift of God's presence.

Writing will help you to engage your actions, beliefs, and patterns of behavior, and to reflect on the ways in which you shelter your heart from being vulnerable to daily life. Just write. Do not edit your words or worry about language or punctuation. If you enter into this process sincerely and prayerfully, this method of prayer will reveal your thoughts, concerns, worries, and fears.

The action statement each day will hopefully come naturally from your reflections and prayers. Use the one offered, or perhaps writing your own will be more helpful. These will mostly not be actions that you complete within your retreat time or even within the Advent season. Rather, these action steps are intended to carry you out into the world as a disciple of Jesus Christ. Consider them first steps in a long process of transformation. Just as we are sent forth from Mass each Sunday to spread the peace of Christ, so these small commitments you make will help guide you in your work on behalf of the Gospel. Allow yourself to be deeply challenged about how you will live what you profess.

Step 5. Prayer: Writing Your Way to New Birth

The section called "Prayer" is offered each day to challenge your thinking about your relationship with God. At the end of each week I offer a prayer, which you may use to begin your own discernment and gather ideas for how to express what is going on in your relationship with God. But keep in mind that the genuine prayer of the retreat will flow from your written responses to the prompts mentioned in the fourth step.

Collect your insights and prayers in this booklet, your own journal, or simply on scrap paper; and take time each day to compose your own prayer. Your written prayers do not need to be formal or follow any particular pattern. They may be just a few words, a sentence or two, or many words. Just write the words God gives you to open your heart. You may even find that your prayer comes without words. Write (if it helps), reflect, and pray in the way that becomes comfortable for you during your daily meditations.

Watch!

SUNDAY

Step 1. Welcome the Stranger Called Silence

Settle into your retreat space and sit in silence for a minute or two.

Step 2. Discover Your Story Within the Word

As you make the sign of the cross, pray:

O God, unshelter my heart that I may hear and know your holy Word.

Read the gospel passage in silence or aloud.

Mark 13:33–37
Jesus said to his disciples: "Be watchful! Be alert! You do not know when the time will come. It is like a man traveling abroad. He leaves home and places his servants in charge, each with his own work, and orders the gatekeeper to be on the watch. Watch, therefore; you do not know when the lord of the house is coming, whether in the evening, or midnight, or at cockcrow, or in the morning. May he not come suddenly and find you sleeping. What I say to you, I say to all: 'Watch!'"

Spend another minute or two in silent reflection.

Step 3. Connect to the Waiting World: Watch!

I fear the nighttime darkness. As the sun sets on downtown Portland, I grow more restless and uncertain. I hear the piercing sirens of ambulances and fire trucks storm the dusk. I wonder who in our neighborhood overdosed on heroin or started a barroom fight. I hear shouts on the street corners as darkness covers the tall buildings, and I realize our local drug dealers are keeping the night watch. I hear cigarette-induced coughing and occasional laughter under my bedroom window and recognize that our friends are staking out a place to sleep in front of our church entrance. I breathe deeply as daylight fades, praying no one will be raped during the night as friends sleep tightly against the church building.

I feel the darkness of night in my own body. My heart is anxious because I heard that one of our friends in a local single-room-occupancy hotel is off his medication. I pray he will not jump out his fifth-story window as his long-time friend did last weekend. My breathing stops as I hear screeches from oversized car tires rumbling to an incomplete stop at the traffic light and know that drug violence on our street corner is close behind. With one eye open, I sleep—just waiting for the sound of gunshot outside my window.

As a gatekeeper of the night, I beg God to cover our friends curled up on the concrete in the cold rain. I pray that our elderly neighbors will not roam the night streets looking for their lost childhoods. I get on my knees to make sure God will not forget people suffering from mental distress and illness because so few people care for them in the daylight. I am a gatekeeper who still cries out at night because so many people feel they do not belong to society or feel welcomed into their families of origin. So many people feel alone and believe they are not sheltered among the healing rays of Christ's love and protection.

It is in my neighborhood darkness that I hear Jesus telling his disciples to be watchful and alert. This darkness is the place where I happen to live; and the cold, bitter night is long and treacherous. I am one of the servants left in charge, and I know I cannot manage all of these situations myself. I cannot change people's minds about feeling lost and abandoned. I cannot control the night sky, nor can I stop the reckless behavior of manic people who cannot afford their medications. As a faithful servant, I must turn to the promise that Christ will remain with us until the end of time. Christ's love breaks into our human loss, tragedy, and sin—into my own feelings of abandonment and uncertainty.

This is the place where Advent begins. This is the real life of all believers who know that darkness is replaced with the light of Christ. I fear the darkness, but I am not alone. People from every walk of life share this nighttime fear. I fear for the young runaway teen outside, covered up with rain-soaked blankets—while a young mother in another city sleeps restlessly, listening to her sick infant girl wrapped in new blankets in a bedroom down the hall. I fear the old man covered with vomit and passed out on the sidewalk—while a doctor serving the suburbs fears for the heart-attack victim who just arrived on the gurney from her seventieth birthday party. An elderly wife sleeps in fear as she cares for her husband with Alzheimer's. A middle-aged widower stays awake all night reminiscing and grieving a tragic loss. A young student pulls another all-nighter because he works two jobs to get through junior college while financially supporting his siblings.

We are all watchers of the gate. We are all waiting for God. The sacred season of Advent begins with the call and words of Christ to make us all ready for the master's return. These urgent words sting our consciences and call us to live with intention and purpose. Christ calls us back to a deeper faith amidst our own responsibilities in life—the people, events, situations, and relationships. These words of Christ unmask our hearts and set our priorities anew. At the beginning of Advent this challenge of Christ offers us a new way of seeing our faith and trusting in the power of God's love, even if life is so incredibly difficult.

My fear does not relent in the dawn. When the long night is over and daylight breaks, the suffering in people's lives continues to reveal itself. People need lasting health care, and they search from one agency to another for short-term remedies. They are sick from long-term diseases of the street—gangrene, diabetes, and high blood pressure. Filled with loneliness, isolation, and worry that no medication can ease or cure, people roam the streets. I watch not only during the long, cold winter nights of December, but also in its short days filled with prejudice, gang violence, and chronic illness. This is the Advent message of watching for Christ's appearance, waiting for life to heal itself in the miracles of God's love and faithfulness.

This new liturgical season begins with us hovering among the shadows of worry, fear, and uncertainty, even though God is present, active, and loving in the world. As believers in the light of Christ, fear of the dark is the common situation in which deep and abiding faith is born in every life, in every neighborhood, in every generation, time, and place. Once again I muster the courage to rouse my nighttime vision of hope and watch diligently amidst people's suffering for the Lord's coming.

Step 4. Respond to the Cry of the Prophets

Christ calls us to watch for the master's return. We are to be ready, alert, and vigilant. This watchfulness, this new awareness of life and faith demands much of us who follow Christ. Advent begins with an urgent command that cannot be ignored. As we look more deeply, we must commit to real effort and prayer to ascertain what this seemingly simple word—*watch*—means for the particulars of our lives.

This year the Gospel of Mark calls forth the fidelity of the gatekeeper, the one who is responsible for keeping intruders away from the property. The gatekeeper helps maintain the safety of other people, and as we listen to the gospel, we are being urged to a new watchfulness in every aspect of our lives. We begin by reflecting on our relationships with the people whom we love.

We will find a deeper reliance on God if we begin to strengthen our prayer for people who depend on us. Whom are we being asked to watch more carefully during this season of Advent? What does it mean for us to watch our children, their talents, ideas, and concerns? How can we strengthen bonds with our aging parents or an ill relative by becoming more vigilant about their daily needs, their health care, or inability to pay for long-term support? How do we watch people with love and gratitude, and not with judgment or harsh words? Christ is calling us to continue watching our relationships with care. He urges us to deepen the bonds of love in our world and to honor those who have been entrusted to our care.

1. Christ is calling me to a deeper trust so that I

2. As Advent begins, I know I must examine my relationships so that

3. Today, I am being called to "watch"

Action: Today I will be quiet and reflect on my important relationships.

Step 5. Prayer: Writing Your Way to New Birth

Take a minute or two to look back at what you have written. Then compose a short prayer offering whatever is in your heart to God. Write it in the space below or in the quiet of your heart and mind.

MONDAY

Step 1. Welcome the Stranger Called Silence

Settle into your retreat space and sit in silence for a minute or two.

Step 2. Discover Your Story Within the Word

As you make the sign of the cross, pray:

O God, unshelter my heart that I may hear and know your holy Word.

Read the Sunday gospel passage (p. 5) in silence or aloud.

Then spend another minute or two in silent reflection on the reading.

For what will you watch today?

Step 3. Connect to the Waiting World: Watch!

You may wish to revisit the thematic essay on pages 6–8 if it will help you focus your retreat time.

Take a couple of minutes to think about how well you did with your action from yesterday. Journal about it if that is useful.

Step 4. Respond to the Cry of the Prophets

Christ will come again when we least expect him. We know neither the day nor the hour. We also live with the assurance that Christ is already in time, in our day, with us at night, and in every place that we are. For every believer, time is eternal: Christ yesterday, today, and forever. However, we also look to the gatekeeper to remind us that, in fact, we live in this present moment, in our particular culture.

The gatekeeper is vigilant at all hours of the day. This urgent warrior seems not to rest, nor to rely on others for help. The image of the gatekeeper reminds us to use our time on earth well, to respect each moment of waiting and longing for God. Our watchfulness is rooted deeply within our faith and the fact that we already know Christ in our relationships, through the people we love intimately, and in our place in the world.

As we enter into the mystery of Advent, how do we use our time for serving others? Do we resist doing something new or out of our comfort zone? Are we stingy with our hours, our encounters, our way of being in the world? Do we resist the stranger, new requests on our schedules, or live a life too "busy" to listen to the needs of people? Do we think we control every hour of the day, or can we rest in the assurance that Christ is in charge of the rising and the setting of the sun as we experience life?

1. I need to reconsider my attitudes about my use of time because

2. As I live today, I trust that God is

3. I describe my attitudes about time as

Action: Today I will be attentive to how I use time.

Step 5. Prayer: Writing Your Way to New Birth

Take a minute or two to look back at what you have written. Then compose a short prayer offering whatever is in your heart to God. Write it in the space below or in the quiet of your heart and mind.

TUESDAY

Step 1. Welcome the Stranger Called Silence

Settle into your retreat space and sit in silence for a minute or two.

Step 2. Discover Your Story Within the Word

As you make the sign of the cross, pray:

O God, unshelter my heart that I may hear and know your holy Word.

Read the Sunday gospel passage in silence or aloud. Then spend another minute or two in silent reflection on the reading.

For what will you watch today?

Step 3. Connect to the Waiting World: Watch!

Reflect on your action from yesterday.

How well have you met that goal?

Step 4. Respond to the Cry of the Prophets

Christ calls us to act courageously, to be intentional in our tasks of waiting and searching for his presence. In Advent, we hear the gospels challenging us to live bravely as believers, bringing the light of Christ to every aspect of life. This moment of courage, this action of fearlessness may catch us off guard. The coming of God into the world does not depend on us, but we are to live with expectancy and thoughtfulness in the presence of God and in longing for Christ's return. This belief demands of us significant trust and courage.

The gatekeeper's job at first glance seems rather boring and uneventful. Waiting is not the easiest chore no matter our background or our place in life. The job of the gatekeeper is more than waiting; it is a courageous action of belief and hope for the gatekeeper and for the people who count on the gatekeeper's perceptions.

The gatekeeper calls each of us into courageous belief and action. Do we have the faith to wait for God? Do we trust enough to rely on God's presence even when God seems most absent in daily life? Do we find within our hearts a true desire for God and the bravery to act on that belief? Do we falter in our efforts to wait for God in the center of our failure, doubt, and mistrust? Our waiting for God is an act of great courage and love.

1. I see my own waiting and searching for God as an act of trust because

2. I pray for deeper courage because I get so weary from

3. God, call me into a deeper and more courageous life so that

Action: Today, I will write in a journal about what really matters to me.

Step 5. Prayer: Writing Your Way to New Birth

Take a minute or two to look back at what you have written. Then compose a short prayer offering whatever is in your heart to God. Write it in the space below or in the quiet of your heart and mind.

WEDNESDAY

Step 1. Welcome the Stranger Called Silence

Settle into your retreat space and sit in silence for a minute or two.

Step 2. Discover Your Story Within the Word

As you make the sign of the cross, pray:

O God, unshelter my heart that I may hear and know your holy Word.

Read the Sunday gospel passage in silence or aloud. Then spend another minute or two in silent reflection on the reading.

For what will you watch today?

Step 3. Connect to the Waiting World: Watch!

Reflect on your action from yesterday.

How well have you met that goal?

Step 4. Respond to the Cry of the Prophets

Christ calls us to watch and wait even when we think our talents are neither sufficient nor trustworthy. We all hear this message during this Advent season. No one is excluded from this challenge Christ is offering. Yet, we may hear the voice of Christ with reluctant hearts, thinking that Christ must be speaking to someone else!

The gatekeeper is the person who tells us that Christ comes in the particular circumstances of each or our lives. We are called into waiting and preparing for Christ no matter our lives, jobs, talents, or gifts. We all live the mission of the gatekeeper, allowing God to transform our human skills into a genuine life of faith, integrity, and hope. Our baptism initiates us into this life of faith and daily prayer and opens our hearts to discover the person of Christ in our unique situations in life. The gatekeeper is not just one person, but we all keep our eyes peeled for Christ, our hearts ready for his return. The gatekeeper is the doorway to the holy.

We are all called to wait for God, even when we think we are incapable. How are you being called to witness God's life during this holy season? What are your God-given gifts, talents, and abilities? How do you use your talents for God's purpose? How do you respect the abilities God has already given you? Each person comes to understand the meaning of Advent, the depth of God's presence within his or her own life.

1. I often judge my abilities out of shame and guilt because

2. God, I know you are asking me to

3. Christ, I wait in the Advent darkness for

Action: Today, I will list my talents and shortcomings.

Step 5. Prayer: Writing Your Way to New Birth

Take a minute or two to look back at what you have written. Then compose a short prayer offering whatever is in your heart to God. Write it in the space below or in the quiet of your heart and mind.

THURSDAY

Step 1. Welcome the Stranger Called Silence

Settle into your retreat space and sit in silence for a minute or two.

Step 2. Discover Your Story Within the Word

As you make the sign of the cross, pray:

O God, unshelter my heart that I may hear and know your holy Word.

Read the Sunday gospel passage in silence or aloud. Then spend another minute or two in silent reflection on the reading.

For what will you watch today?

Step 3. Connect to the Waiting World: Watch!

Reflect on your action from yesterday.

How well have you met that goal?

Step 4. Respond to the Cry of the Prophets

Christ is the source of genuine welcome and hospitality. When Jesus entered the human condition, becoming flesh for us, he opened his divine life to every person. The Incarnation, God-among-us, is the model for every believer to welcome the stranger and the outcast. Jesus' presence among us gives us a hope for new life for all people.

The gatekeeper expresses deep longing as the gate is opened to the stranger. The gatekeeper welcomes the unexpected person as well as yearning for the master's return. We also welcome the stranger into our lives every day as we see within the stranger's eyes the person of our desire, the person of Christ Jesus. The gatekeeper opens us to the divine in each person if we are willing to see this mystery for ourselves.

As we progress through Advent, how do you welcome the strangers around you? How do you welcome and accept each person as a divine gift? Welcoming the stranger or even people we love often brings guilt, uncertainty, or even fear. How do you release yourself from false judgment or rigid opinion of the stranger? How can you see within the eyes of the other person the divine person of Christ? Advent becomes for us a time of new hospitality and new longing for the people around us as well as the hungry, the lost, and the forgotten. Within the life of a stranger, we can often discover our own deep longing for the divine.

1. I experience genuine hospitality when

2. I find it difficult to welcome a person into my life when

3. When I meet a stranger, I often discover Christ if I

Action: Today, I will pay attention to how I engage a stranger.

Step 5. Prayer: Writing Your Way to New Birth

Take a minute or two to look back at what you have written. Then compose a short prayer offering whatever is in your heart to God. Write it in the space below or in the quiet of your heart and mind.

FRIDAY

Step 1. Welcome the Stranger Called Silence

Settle into your retreat space and sit in silence for a minute or two.

Step 2. Discover Your Story Within the Word

As you make the sign of the cross, pray:

O God, unshelter my heart that I may hear and know your holy Word.

Read the Sunday gospel passage in silence or aloud. Then spend another minute or two in silent reflection on the reading.

For what will you watch today?

Step 3. Connect to the Waiting World: Watch!

Reflect on your action from yesterday.

How well have you met that goal?

Step 4. Respond to the Cry of the Prophets

Christ comes among us when we are exhausted from waiting and searching for change. Christ reveals love among us in every moment of life; but we may become full of fear from aging, ill health, or the numerous demands placed on our lives. The invitation is always before us, but we may be too numb from empty promises or too exhausted to live for something new.

Again, the icon of the gatekeeper models fidelity in the search. The scriptures capture this ageless set of eyes peering with delight on the master's return. In our real lives, our eyes may be red from sheer exhaustion and full of tears, wondering what our waiting for God really means. The gatekeeper seems to show us that no matter our age, our state of health, or the money we possess, the waiting is worth the time and energy.

Nearing the end of the first week of Advent, take stock of your life and all the demands put on you by others. How can you focus on this Advent journey in the midst of being tired, afraid, or lonely? How can you offer your search for others who have grown weary from apathy, advanced age, or another deeply felt hardship? These questions remind us that Advent arrives in the emotional places of our honest lives. Christ is waiting for us whether or not we are eager or awake to discover him.

1. So much is demanded of me in these Advent days, so I

2. I am really not focused on my own spiritual journey, and I need

3. Jesus, receive me as I am and

Action: Today, I will notice what makes me tired and afraid.

Step 5. Prayer: Writing Your Way to New Birth

Take a minute or two to look back at what you have written. Then compose a short prayer offering whatever is in your heart to God. Write it in the space below or in the quiet of your heart and mind.

SATURDAY

Step 1. Welcome the Stranger Called Silence

Settle into your retreat space and sit in silence for a minute or two.

Step 2. Discover Your Story Within the Word

As you make the sign of the cross, pray:

O God, unshelter my heart that I may hear and know your holy Word.

Read the Sunday gospel passage in silence or aloud. Then spend another minute or two in silent reflection on the reading.

For what will you watch today?

Step 3. Connect to the Waiting World: Watch!

Reflect on your action from yesterday.

How well have you met that goal?

Step 4. Respond to the Cry of the Prophets

Christ asks us to cultivate within our hearts a deep desire for God. This is a fundamental aspect of Advent. Our common waiting, preparing, and longing instill within our hearts a fire for the real presence of Christ. The Incarnation forms us into the people of God. With ready hearts, open minds, a sincere presence, and endless patience, we wait for the second coming of Christ.

The face of the gatekeeper reveals a longing for the master's return. This arrival will be a time of rejoicing and love. Love builds a desire within all of us to allow room in our hearts for Christ's return. God's love finds a home within our longing.

For what do we genuinely long in this season of Advent? We are confronted with many advertisements, family and cultural expectations, and our society's economic bottom line. Our real longing is often hidden—even from ourselves. Our scurrying around to please other people or our own lack of self-worth shields us from how much we truly desire the master, the very love of God. Take the time you need—as no one can accomplish this for you—to be with God in prayer. In time, God will reveal to you the golden desire of love itself, the Lord's real presence among us.

1. I seem to be numb to my own needs at this time in life, and so I

2. I ache to find my own heart in God's desire, and so

3. Jesus, find me in your love for all people and

Action: Today, I will pay attention to what I most desire in life.

Step 5. Prayer: Writing Your Way to New Birth

Take a minute or two to look back at what you have written. Then compose a short prayer offering whatever is in your heart to God. Write it in the space below or in the quiet of your heart and mind.

Prayer for the First Week of Advent

I ran out of the parish building last Tuesday to drive to the grocery store.
My gaze fell upon a friend wrapped in layers of clothing.
Jesus, I stared at Tom rummaging through the city trash container.
He struggled to squeeze his naked hand into the dirty bin.

His childlike face lit up as if his hand were stuck in a cookie jar.
I watched him search for morsels and scraps. I intruded on his dinnertime.
He has been surviving, living outside for a very long time.
No trip to the market, no feast with friends tonight for Tom.

Jesus, I watched him, and my mind flashed back to last Easter.
You welcomed him into the Church during the Easter Vigil.
His hands were open and clean that night.
He received his daily bread and his place among us.

Jesus, assure Tom that he still belongs among us fragile ones.
Open our hands to welcome and feed him.
Jesus, we all wait for you in the night.

Amen.

Seek Messengers of Hope

SUNDAY

Step 1. Welcome the Stranger Called Silence

Settle into your retreat space and sit in silence for a minute or two.

Step 2. Discover Your Story Within the Word

As you make the sign of the cross, pray:

O God, unshelter my heart that I may hear and know your holy Word.

Read the Sunday gospel passage in silence or aloud.

Mark 1:1–8
The beginning of the gospel of Jesus Christ the Son of God. As it is written in Isaiah the prophet: Behold, I am sending my messenger ahead of you; he will prepare your way. A voice of the one crying out in the desert: "Prepare the way of the Lord, make straight his paths." John the Baptist appeared in the desert proclaiming a baptism of repentance for the forgiveness of sins. People of the whole of Judean countryside and all of the inhabitants of Jerusalem were going out to him

and were being baptized by him in the Jordan River as they acknowledged their sins. John was clothed in camel's hair, with a leather belt around his waist. He fed on locusts and wild honey. And this is what he proclaimed: "One mightier than I is coming after me. I am not worthy to stoop and loosen the thongs of his sandals. I have baptized you with water; he will baptize you with the Holy Spirit."

Spend another minute or two in silent reflection on the reading.

Step 3. Connect to the Waiting World: Seek Messengers of Hope

I beg God for a messenger of hope in our neighborhood. As we begin the second Sunday of Advent, John the Baptist is identified as God's messenger. John carries the message of love, reform, and commitment well beyond the desert, well beyond ancient times. I pray that John's strong influence will be heard in our neighborhood, that a message of change will be received by people living in this generation of dread, sorrow, and uncertainty.

I witness messengers of various kinds on our streets. Hooded drug dealers roam the wet sidewalks, hiding out in dark doorways waiting for business. Strangers driving sleek cars with amplified mufflers steer slowly around the block over and over again in the night. Young women wearing caked makeup to mask their anger, pain, and abuse mosey slowly around the block, stumbling out of their high-heeled shoes. I overhear grunts, shouting, and commands from all these streetwalkers, and I realize they are all receiving messages from one another. Everyone is waiting for the urgent message of the next deal, trick, or hit.

The deeper message being received by so many people on our block is that their lives do not matter. Some people never feel welcome in their own skin. The runaway teen prostitute is merely living out the messages that she received as a child, that her presence in the world does not make a difference to anyone. Heroin, cocaine, and alcohol become welcomed messengers of numbness, disassociation, and escape. These messages need drastic healing, a new voice of hope in our broken neighborhood.

Outside our parish doors, shopping carts piled high with possessions and covered with plastic tarps are loosely tied to bicycle racks. Their owners sleep the night away huddled around the perimeter of our building. They rest under the bright lights in our entryway in order to feel safe in the long winter night. The messages that these night-warriors face are that they do not deserve care and consolation. Years of mental illness have worn many of them down into fear, hopelessness, and rage. People walk by these sleeping neighbors and spit in their faces, rummage through their carts, and steal their dignity. These messages repeat themselves in Advent and through every dark night of the year.

I sit listening to the bitter wind whip its way around the corner and hear it whistling through my unlatched windows. I breathe deeply and realize the contrast with my sheltered life—my dry room, clean clothes, and more-than-enough food to eat. I feel the contradiction of my over-abundance with my religious vow of poverty. My heart clings way too tightly to my physical possessions. During Advent, my pampered life as a priest speaks a message that causes me discomfort.

I become aware of my inner conflict even more when our parish staff is unable to respond positively to many people's needs. We do not have enough diapers for the newborn infant tucked away in layers of blankets in a makeshift stroller. We do not have an extra blanket or a heavy jacket for the young man who was just released from jail last night. We are out of feminine hygiene products for the runaway tattooed teen with the large ring piercing her nose. Unfortunately, we do not always have what people need. For people in need, this simple reality is translated into there not being enough love to go around. This is the same message they have heard their entire lives.

I realize our block is not the only lonely place. The elderly widower still living on the family farm worries that some day he will no longer be capable of driving his truck to get his only daily meal. The bashful young boy cringes going out to recess because he is bullied, and even his friends will not snitch on the perpetrator. The stay-at-home mother frets that she will be caught hiding her liquor in a basement closet. The athletic, professionally successful young father rages against his teenage daughter and finally realizes he has pushed her away. These are all the places of profound loneliness that are in need of John's message that something new will happen in everyone's life when we wait for God alone.

This second Sunday of Advent challenges us to acknowledge the messages in our lives that need redemption. We are all placed within the sound of John's strong and piercing voice, which promises that new paths will become a straight line to God's love and goodness. John's influence will open our hearts—if we have the courage to live differently, to live deeply within the call of God. His message is one that will take us into people's suffering, into their deep fear and loneliness. In this Advent season, we all are called to open our hearts to a new message of justice, love, and communion.

We all belong within the sound of John's call to wait for love. John's insistence that we reorder our lives, come to grips with our past, and hope for the future rests in the hearts of all people. I live among so many people who can never believe that God is truly for them. My challenge is to respond to the raw needs of people everywhere, beginning within my own neighborhood. This week I prepare my own heart to be open, caring, and available for Christ Jesus.

Step 4. Respond to the Cry of the Prophets

John the Baptist sprints through the desert, demanding that our attention remain centered on Christ Jesus. John proclaims this message of urgency to all believers. He is courageous, strong, and dedicated to the message that all people belong in Christ. These consoling words come from God, but we may not be ready to receive their message. We may feel unworthy of this invitation or feel judged by other believers. Some people are put down by others' self-righteousness or feel slammed by messages of failure, inadequacy, or prejudice.

The beginning of Mark's gospel challenges us to be ready for Christ's return. Jesus' cousin John is proclaiming not only his family loyalty but also a new vision of the world. John desires that all people hear the call for conversion and change so that we understand within our hearts the person of Christ Jesus. The word of God fashions us not in judgment or violence in this world, but jolts us out of our complacency so that we will rest in the security and assurance of love here and now. John's message stirs up the sands of the desert and the storms of our own self-doubt.

During this second week of Advent, what messages do you hear about your life that need redemption or new life? We all are bombarded with messages of hatred, neglect, self-preservation, and dishonesty. How can you separate yourself from many of these negative messages? How can you pray through the negative in order to discover the hope of Christ Jesus? The Gospel of Mark prepares us to receive a new message of hope and reform in the kingdom of God. Our common prayer opens us all to participate here on earth in the real message of Christ's love.

1. The negative messages that seem to bind my heart and life now are

2. I pray during this season of Advent that I will become a messenger of

3. I hear John's invitation, and I feel

Action: Today, I will pay attention to the conflicting messages of the season.

Step 5. Prayer: Writing Your Way to New Birth

Take a minute or two to look back at what you have written. Then compose a short prayer offering whatever is in your heart to God. Write it in the space below or in the quiet of your heart and mind.

MONDAY

Step 1. Welcome the Stranger Called Silence

Settle into your retreat space and sit in silence for a minute or two.

Step 2. Discover Your Story Within the Word

As you make the sign of the cross, pray:

O God, unshelter my heart that I may hear and know your holy Word.

Read the Sunday gospel passage (pp. 23–24) in silence or aloud. Then spend another minute or two in silent reflection on the reading.

What emotional and spiritual pathways can you clear for Christ's coming this day?

Step 3. Connect to the Waiting World: Seek Messengers of Hope

You may wish to revisit the thematic essay on pages 24–26 if it will help you focus your retreat time.

Take a couple of minutes to think about how well you did with your action from yesterday. Journal about it if that is useful.

Step 4. Respond to the Cry of the Prophets

John exudes confidence in preparing us for Christ. He has found the path of love for his own life. Living this intensity is never easy. We may hear John's message of preparation but feel that our lives do not count among the chosen, the powerful, or the beautiful.

Sometimes our path in life is not so easy to determine. Our lives seem to be full of crooked paths and narrow escapes. We may not understand or appreciate our own gifts, talents, and desires.

The season of Advent encourages each person to rest in the assurance that Christ is present on earth for all people. These weeks leading up to the celebration of Christmas are not meant to be an affirmation of wealth, prosperity, and health. These weeks challenge us to live for people who struggle in life, who find their own lives cloudy with self-doubt. Advent attunes our ears not only to John's piercing voice, but to the message of love and compassion in Christ Jesus.

John's message is meant to rest in the heart of fragile and lonely people. As you all hear this week's gospel reading again, how do you embrace the message from John that you belong to God always? How can you begin to bear this message for people around you? How are you being called to live differently because of this message? At times, we all feel far from this message. How will you be convinced that God is on your side, has your interests in mind, and loves you just as you are?

1. In this Advent season, the despairing message of my life seems

2. I hold on to the power of God to change my past so

3. God, receive me as I am and call me to

Action: Today, I will pay attention to the conflicting messages within me.

Step 5. Prayer: Writing Your Way to New Birth

Take a minute or two to look back at what you have written. Then compose a short prayer offering whatever is in your heart to God. Write it in the space below or in the quiet of your heart and mind.

TUESDAY

Step 1. Welcome the Stranger Called Silence

Settle into your retreat space and sit in silence for a minute or two.

Step 2. Discover Your Story Within the Word

As you make the sign of the cross, pray:

O God, unshelter my heart that I may hear and know your holy Word.

Read the Sunday gospel passage in silence or aloud. Then spend another minute or two in silent reflection on the reading.

What emotional and spiritual pathways can you clear for Christ's coming this day?

Step 3. Connect to the Waiting World: Seek Messengers of Hope

Reflect on your action from yesterday.

How well have you met that goal?

Step 4. Respond to the Cry of the Prophets

Many people heard the sound of John's voice and heeded his plea to follow. They were drawn to his message because of his conviction and certainty. So many people wanted to belong to God. They were going out to the desert to meet him and to discover something more about their own lives. They left the security of their lives and their past, and waited with John the Baptist for something new.

Advent is also a spiritual journey for all of us, for people who set their hearts on God's kingdom. This journey does not mean that we will follow John out into the desert, but it may signify our wandering into places of loneliness, isolation, and conversion. The deserts of today very well may be our local hospitals, our neighborhood nursing homes, or our children's schools in need of repairs and better-paid teachers. Perhaps the deserts of our day are our suburban malls where our teenagers are being trafficked for sex and drugs. There are many deserts where John's voice needs to ring out for non-violence and respect for all life.

The message of John may not always attract followers to the deserts of our day. In fact, some people may be repelled by such a message. How can you keep John's message of conversion alive in the particular circumstances of your life? How firmly do you believe that John's call to change is real preparation for the coming of Christ in every life? We all must find our place among the people who ran out to meet John, because his message is really about every person belonging in the presence of the Savior. How can you be open and ready to receive the message of profound love within your life?

1. God, help me spread the word of hope to

2. The negative message that I carry within me is

3. God, help me on my Advent journey to understand

Action: Today, I will admit the negative messages I continue to pass on to others.

Step 5. Prayer: Writing Your Way to New Birth

Take a minute or two to look back at what you have written. Then compose a short prayer offering whatever is in your heart to God. Write it in the space below or in the quiet of your heart and mind.

WEDNESDAY

Step 1. Welcome the Stranger Called Silence

Settle into your retreat space and sit in silence for a minute or two.

Step 2. Discover Your Story Within the Word

As you make the sign of the cross, pray:

O God, unshelter my heart that I may hear and know your holy Word.

Read the Sunday gospel passage in silence or aloud. Then spend another minute or two in silent reflection on the reading.

What emotional and spiritual pathways can you clear for Christ's coming this day?

Step 3. Connect to the Waiting World: Seek the Messengers of Hope

Reflect on your action from yesterday.

How well have you met that goal?

Step 4. Respond to the Cry of the Prophets

Many people who followed John were likely dissatisfied with their lives. Perhaps they found a shallowness that could be filled only by God's grace. Certainly, some were so used to the negative messages of their lives, such as not feeling loved nor feeling part of the plan of God's kingdom. As I meet people in ministry, I realize that hardship and loneliness create a deep ache for healing and communion. People today long for the same message sought by John's followers. We all need to change our ways, to open new doors to God, to be released from the sin and doubt that befalls even the most dedicated follower.

The Advent season cultivates within our hearts a deep and passionate desire for love. Only God's love will ultimately sustain us. Unfortunately, this season of great expectations and displays of wealth also creates within us a profound loneliness. There is a real and powerful realization by so many people in the world that they will never find the love they truly desire. This is a very complicated aspect of the Advent and Christmas season that needs to be talked about in families and in faith communities. The promise of God touches our most profound loneliness; yet, so many people give up trying because both God and other people seem so far away from their lives.

How can we you enter into John's message of conversion and change during this Advent season? How can you sustain your life in God's presence during this liturgical season? How can you be an instrument of grace, forgiveness, and love? Every believer longs to move out of a realm of dissatisfaction into a rich and joyful relationship with God. This movement out of loneliness takes time, grace, and much support for many people.

1. Jesus, I long for

2. I seek God's forgiveness in my life in the area of

3. The message of Advent that I desire to pass on to other people is

Action: Today, I will pray for those who are lonely and confront my own loneliness.

Step 5. Prayer: Writing Your Way to New Birth

Take a minute or two to look back at what you have written. Then compose a short prayer offering whatever is in your heart to God. Write it in the space below or in the quiet of your heart and mind.

THURSDAY

Step 1. Welcome the Stranger Called Silence

Settle into your retreat space and sit in silence for a minute or two.

Step 2. Discover Your Story Within the Word

As you make the sign of the cross, pray:

O God, unshelter my heart that I may hear and know your holy Word.

Read the Sunday gospel passage in silence or aloud. Then spend another minute or two in silent reflection on the reading.

What emotional and spiritual pathways can you clear for Christ's coming this day?

Step 3. Connect to the Waiting World: Seek the Messengers of Hope

Reflect on your action from yesterday.

How well have you met that goal?

Step 4. Respond to the Cry of the Prophets

John's message of reform and conversion was also stark and simple. In fact, the message and the messenger were united. John's stark appearance, wearing camel hair and a leather belt, spoke of his honest approach to conversion, his priority in God. He placed his trust in God even for the basics of food and clothing. His appearance still challenges us in our profound consumerism, convenience-driven lifestyles, and indulgent complacency. The message of rooting our identity and all of our satisfactions in God is certainly countercultural.

As we prepare for Christmas, we often find it difficult to live this priority of simplicity. Unfortunately, the way we celebrate the season and its cultural priorities leaves out many people who cannot afford even modest gifts or comfortable lifestyles during this season. Many people feel they do not belong because they cannot afford all the commercial trappings of Christmas and do not know the comfort of financial stability. They grow angry, despairing, and increasingly isolated. The prophet's message of reform and conversion, which might bring justice to these people in need, cannot become lost amid holiday sugar highs and hangovers. True longing for God and the kingdom of peace cannot be met by acquiring new gadgets, luxury food items, or the latest fashions.

How do you try to keep the authentic message of God alive during Advent? How do you live a genuine life that speaks for itself of God's priorities? What is the purpose of your faith and a life that welcomes all people regardless of what they may or may not possess? The answers to these questions will cultivate a rich faith and brand-new discovery of God if we receive John's message with an open and unsheltered heart.

1. Jesus, I prepare to receive your forgiving love by

2. I long to simplify my life, but I

3. God, reveal a rich and sustaining desire for faith in me as I

Action: Today, I will make an honest appraisal of my possessions.

Step 5. Prayer: Writing Your Way to New Birth

Take a minute or two to look back at what you have written. Then compose a short prayer offering whatever is in your heart to God. Write it in the space below or in the quiet of your heart and mind.

FRIDAY

Step 1. Welcome the Stranger Called Silence

Settle into your retreat space and sit in silence for a minute or two.

Step 2. Discover Your Story Within the Word

As you make the sign of the cross, pray:

O God, unshelter my heart that I may hear and know your holy Word.

Read the Sunday gospel passage in silence or aloud. Then spend another minute or two in silent reflection on the reading.

What emotional and spiritual pathways can you clear for Christ's coming this day?

Step 3. Connect to the Waiting World: Seek Messengers of Hope

Reflect on your action from yesterday.

How well have you met that goal?

Step 4. Respond to the Cry of the Prophets

As we celebrate the Eucharist this Advent, we focus on our communion with the world, with every person and circumstance. The invitation to gather at the same table unifies our lives as members of families and of the Church. Providing daily food for others is also an extension of the Eucharist. Ladling soup in a homeless shelter, offering a handout on a street corner, sharing cookies in a nursery school, or buying breakfast for a new coworker extends our communion of love in the world. John the Baptist understood that God alone feeds us, no matter our deepest hungers. He proclaimed the richness of the kingdom of God even with the simplicity of eating locusts and wild honey.

Our dinner parties or simple refreshments during this season remind us of our communion with people. We may visit briefly with strangers or sit around a table with family for hours telling stories of the past. We may find our deep communion with a blind date or our aging parents. We build relationships with people through eating, dining, and sharing our lives. Our celebrations with food invite us to share wisdom with our children, reminisce with our long-distant relatives, or reestablish bonds of friendship with college roommates.

In this Advent season, our priority to discover people while sharing our common food is so important. Whom will you welcome to your holiday feast? Who are you reluctant to celebrate with or hesitant to sit next to at Christmas dinner? Who are the people excluded from your parish gatherings, family dinners, or office luncheons? What relationships need mending over a glass of wine and an honest conversation? All of our relationships need the support and love of sharing food and honest conversation.

1. During this Advent season, I look forward to reminiscing with

2. I will mend some of my family relationships this year by

3. I will be honest about my expectations that even sharing a meal may not mend all the hurts I caused by

Action: Today, I will invite a friend to dine with me.

Step 5. Prayer: Writing Your Way to New Birth

Take a minute or two to look back at what you have written. Then compose a short prayer offering whatever is in your heart to God. Write it in the space below or in the quiet of your heart and mind.

SATURDAY

Step 1. Welcome the Stranger Called Silence

Settle into your retreat space and sit in silence for a minute or two.

Step 2. Discover Your Story Within the Word

As you make the sign of the cross, pray:

O God, unshelter my heart that I may hear and know your holy Word.

Read the Sunday gospel passage in silence or aloud. Then spend another minute or two in silent reflection on the reading.

What emotional and spiritual pathways can you clear for Christ's coming this day?

Step 3. Connect to the Waiting World: Seek Messengers of Hope

Reflect on your action from yesterday.

How well have you met that goal?

Step 4. Respond to the Cry of the Prophets

John the Baptist's humble message of conversion and change echoes into our own lives. He pointed to a mightier power, a greater love; he directed everyone to the person of Jesus. This posture of humility teaches us during our celebration of Advent that we are not in charge of the message of hope. We are only instruments of justice. We are part of God's plan that will not be complete in our lifetime.

As we end the second week of Advent, the message of love we carry within our hearts must be clear and decisive. People depend on us to be instruments of God's profound message of hope and freedom, and we must let God be in charge of this revelation. The humble stance of submission required in this will sometimes leave us disappointed with how life works out for us. We may become very frustrated with the Church and cynical about our families. We may carry a deep sense that God's love is not present in our hurt, envy, jealousy, or in our pride.

How can you let God's plan better unfold in you? How does one learn to step into a hurtful or broken situation and offer help, being patient with God to heal the situation? How does one come to understand the difference between working from our pride and being servants of God? How can you rest in God and allow God to do the work of salvation? The continuing story of God's plan is revealed within all humanity. Advent helps us rejoice in this saving message.

1. In my loneliness, I long to receive a message of

2. God, create in me an open heart so that

3. God, the message of healing that the world most needs to hear is

Action: Beginning today, I will offer a message of hope to someone in need.

Step 5. Prayer: Writing Your Way to New Birth

Take a minute or two to look back at what you have written. Then compose a short prayer offering whatever is in your heart to God. Write it in the space below or in the quiet of your heart and mind.

Prayer for the Second Week in Advent

I unloaded my shopping cart at the food market yesterday.
Three people were ahead of me at the checkout counter.
An elderly woman slowly put coins into the hands of the cashier.

Jesus, I recognized her from the hospital bedside of her mentally ill son.
The mother is deaf, and the cashier smiled and signed her words.
The woman bundled in black dropped one of her coins.

As she stood up she caught sight of me at the end of the line.
She grabbed her overstuffed bag of groceries and turned in my direction.
She marked her head with the sign of the cross.

With that gesture she acknowledged where she had met me.
I nodded and smiled. Her fingers flung around her head.
I got the message that her son is still struggling with his mental illness.
He still receives messages that he needs to commit suicide.

Jesus, unravel the torturous messages of fear in him.
Relieve the uncertainty of an elderly mother unable to hear consolation.
Jesus, I received a message of kindness even though I cannot sign my gratitude.

Amen.

Testify to the Light

SUNDAY

Step 1. Welcome the Stranger Called Silence

Settle into your retreat space and sit in silence for a minute or two.

Step 2. Discover Your Story Within the Word

As you make the sign of the cross, pray:

O God, unshelter my heart that I may hear and know your holy Word.

Read the Sunday gospel passage in silence or aloud.

John 1:6–8, 19–28

A man named John was sent from God. He came for testimony, to testify to the light, so that all might believe through him. He was not the light, but came to testify to the light.

And this is the testimony of John. When the Jews from Jerusalem sent priests and Levites to him to ask him, "Who are you?" he admitted and did not deny it, but admitted, "I am not the Christ." So they asked him, "What are you then? Are you Elijah?" And he said, "I

am not." "Are you the Prophet?" He answered, "No." So they said to him, "Who are you, so we can give an answer to those who sent us? What do you have to say for yourself?" He said: "I am the voice of the one crying out in the desert, make straight the way of the Lord, as Isaiah the prophet said." Some of the Pharisees were also sent. They asked him, "Why then do you baptize if you are not the Christ or Elijah or the Prophet?" John answered them, "I baptize you with water; but there is one among you whom you do not recognize, the one who is coming after me, whose sandal strap I am not worthy to untie."
This happened in Bethany across the Jordan, where John was baptizing.

Spend another minute or two in silent reflection on the reading.

Step 3. Connect to the Waiting World: Testify to the Light

I remain restless as I hear the legion of stories that have been muddied by family violence and marred by many years of undiagnosed and untreated mental illness. These voices speak in the short daylight hours of Advent and even ring out in my dreams in the long, cold nights. I listen with my entire being to the young mother, barely out of her teens, as she relives her story of the rape, torture, and violence she endured living with her new husband. My ears will never be fully attuned to the greasy-haired elderly gentleman suffering from Parkinson's disease as he recaps his war experiences over and over again.

The unrelenting voices of people surviving poverty echo in my own heart and wear down my defenses of apathy and indifference. These chaotic voices of people in need expose my own heart to the suffering of people in today's world. And these voices form the core of the liturgical season of Advent. The roar of the ancient prophets in scripture amplifies these human voices of suffering. John the Baptist sounds the call of immediate reform, lasting change, and burning attention to the voices most in need of the message that Christ is coming. John's heralding reform recalls past injustices. His ringing voice still clings to our consciences today, asking us to reform every aspect of social injustice, prejudice, poverty, and corruption.

John's echoing challenges in the desert are heard on the harsh, brutal sidewalks of our urban parish. The voices of people surviving poverty connect me to the real meaning of the Advent season. These street prophets speak boldly of tales I cannot shy away from, neglect, nor shun. These stark voices ring true even on the days when I think I can no longer listen or pay attention to such suffering. The powerless cries of people who have lost jobs, their few belongings, and all relationships teach me the value of my own voice that gives me the chance to testify to the coming light of Christ.

I take to heart the cries of God's beloved. These encounters and interactions form my own voice and place among the faithful. I realize how fragile my own voice can become when I do not pay attention to the needs of others. My voice turns in on itself and I speak then more about my own selfishness, loneliness, and lack of hope. My own restless voice speaks boldly about God's love and compassion when I am faced with other people's daily needs of soap and shampoo, clean underwear, and new socks. When I shut out the voices of people in real need, I catch myself complaining about my own lack of intimacy, my own fears about the future, and my own isolated heart.

John the Baptist's cry comes to us not just blowing in the wind or in abstract ways, but in the circumstances of ordinary life. I cannot pass by the grimy homeless man who sits on the street without hearing John's testimony that all humanity is in need of hope for survival and food for today. I cannot sit at the bedside of a young man dying of AIDS without hearing his burning hope that someday he will be accepted, loved, and forgiven by his family. In Advent, the horrific grief of a mother facing a miscarriage, a neighbor losing his only son to suicide, or a coworker's daughter drugged and raped during her freshman year at college challenge all of us to depend on Christ. All life is pregnant with the voice of John calling for integrity, honesty, and deep faith.

Some people listen to John's desert plea and name his cries for reform as hollow bellowing and caterwauling. Many of our privileged neighbors blame people who live outside for being homeless. They shout back at people who profess their need for help; they call them lazy, degenerate bums, or dopers, and condemn them as a burden on society. We all fear that our money, homes, health, and relationships will be taken from us. We cannot use our voices of power to blame people who have no voice in society because of their plight in life. I dare not blame the young man who was severely sexually and emotionally abused by his father for his depression as an adult. I cannot point the finger of blame at the middle-aged woman who never had a job because she has never received treatment and therapy for her schizophrenia.

When our voices unite, a new gratitude is generated among all who believe in God. This is how John's crying out in the desert leads us to Christ. This is the real message of the third Sunday of Advent—that our voices must unite in a common refrain of gratitude for life and join in testifying to the light of Christ—even when our lives have not turned out as we hoped. Gratitude is a deep gift of faith. Gratitude unites our lives as we silence the name-calling and hush our judgments of other people. Our expression of gratitude is the beginning of Christ's birth in our midst, new life for every human sorrow.

We all can easily ignore the prophetic voices of Advent. The ancient voices of scriptural prophets and the ever-present cries of God's people in poverty rattle all our preparations for Christmas. The serious language from the prophets is easily silenced underneath the familiar joyous carols of the season and loud parties with coworkers. We so often prefer to keep Christmas soft, comfortable, childlike, and whimsical rather than learn to live our faith as adult believers. Adult Christianity means we all must hear the sacred cries of the poor and respond as people bearing hope, kindness, and reform. We must unleash our compassion so that love may be born again in our time, among our commitments, and for each person in every generation.

Step 4. Respond to the Cry of the Prophets

On this third Sunday of Advent we rally around the voice of John the Baptist in order to discover the Christ of our seeking. We are more than halfway to the celebration of the Incarnation, of God-made-flesh. Our celebration takes on a subtle sense of rejoicing. We rejoice in the Christ who is already here, and yet our liturgical prayer, hymns, and scriptures teach us to wait and deepen our desire for God. Christ is in the depths of our lives already. We glimpse him in the contagious excitement of children as they anticipate familiar traditions, gift giving, parties, treats and school holidays. But we do not fully voice our joy as a community of believers until the moment of Christmas.

We know that Advent time is essential to our spiritual lives. We will always face new obstacles that intensify our need for God, and every one of us will come to face a new loneliness that will demand an even deeper dependency on God. We feel the rumbling of jubilation during Advent, and yet we wait with great patience and profound prayer in hope of Christ's revelation of love.

We will never voice true joy in our lives without finding the profound love of God for us. Our common joy is strengthened when we reach out to people who are without true peace or sustaining hope. How can you elevate your own or another's despair and discouragement into a voice of gratitude and joy? How can you help meet the needs of someone who longs for healing or who lacks the material essentials of a decent life, such as food, housing, or shoes? Today our voices are subdued with reverent joy as we wait to fully rejoice in Christ's Incarnation.

1. So far in my life, I depend on God to heal

2. My relationship with God gives me the joy of

3. I rejoice as I hear John's call to

Action: I will testify to the light of Christ by voicing joy and gratitude.

Step 5. Prayer: Writing Your Way to New Birth

Take a minute or two to look back at what you have written. Then compose a short prayer offering whatever is in your heart to God. Write it in the space below or in the quiet of your heart and mind.

MONDAY

Step 1. Welcome the Stranger Called Silence

Settle into your retreat space and sit in silence for a minute or two.

Step 2. Discover Your Story Within the Word

As you make the sign of the cross, pray:

O God, unshelter my heart that I may hear and know your holy Word.

Read the Sunday gospel passage (pp. 43–44) in silence or aloud. Then spend another minute or two in silent reflection on the reading.

In what specific ways will you testify to the light of Christ's presence today?

Step 3. Connect to the Waiting World: Testify to the Light

You may wish to revisit the thematic essay on pages 44–46 if it will help you focus your retreat time.

Take a couple of minutes to think about how well you did with your action from yesterday. Journal about it if that is useful.

Step 4. Respond to the Cry of the Prophets

John lived a life of integrity because he knew that his voice depended on God working within him, and his authentic message still echoes across the centuries. He knew exactly what his role was in God's plan. Our place in God is not always so obvious. However, our voices that clamor for justice are needed just as much as was

John's piercing voice in the desert. We are to strengthen our own voices during this Advent season. This is our way of testifying to the light of justice, love, and gospel commitment. This takes time, growth, and courage.

As believers we may be surprised at the various voices that challenge us during Advent. Any voice that harkens from the desert of poverty, illness, disease, or catastrophe challenges the status quo. However, these surprising voices may be just the ones that wake us from our selfish and sleepy ways. These voices can then become a real source of grace so that we may pursue the God of authentic peace.

I invite you to take John's challenging voice to heart. Sit with his sense of integrity and raw experience of God. Walk into the desert with him and listen to his voice. How are you voicing your own relationship with God during this Advent season? What are the voices of despair that jolt you from your naïveté about people's lives? What do you need to hear this Advent so you may be willing to offer consolation and hope to other people? We hear many competing voices each day; some offer deep personal understanding, and some cut us to the core and cause great pain. Sort out the authentic voices in your life and among your relationships, and listen with your entire being.

1. I hear John's voice of purpose and integrity, and I feel

2. I long to hear a healing voice of

3. God, receive my weak voice of impatience because I

Action: Today, I will take stock of my life and the choices I make.

Step 5. Prayer: Writing Your Way to New Birth

Take a minute or two to look back at what you have written. Then compose a short prayer offering whatever is in your heart to God. Write it in the space below or in the quiet of your heart and mind.

TUESDAY

Step 1. Welcome the Stranger Called Silence

Settle into your retreat space and sit in silence for a minute or two.

Step 2. Discover Your Story Within the Word

As you make the sign of the cross, pray:

O God, unshelter my heart that I may hear and know your holy Word.

Read the Sunday gospel passage in silence or aloud. Then spend another minute or two in silent reflection on the reading.

In what specific ways will you testify to the light of Christ's presence today?

Step 3. Connect to the Waiting World: Testify to the Light

Reflect on your action from yesterday.

How well have you met that goal?

Step 4. Respond to the Cry of the Prophets

John admitted to the priests and Levites that he was the voice crying out in the desert. John's voice became a herald for God but also for a new belonging for people whose voices are still buried by injustice. Advent gives rise to voices that have been silenced by years of hatred, violence, and neglect. These voices of yearning come from prisoners with long-term sentences, orphaned children in neighborhood slums, and people suffering in nursing homes from life-long disabilities. These voices of sheer need so often fall on deaf ears. Or perhaps we hear but do not respond because we fear that our own voices may be silenced if we get too close to tragic human suffering.

The voice of John the Baptist rings clearly in our present age to tell us that we also belong to people whose voices are compromised by poverty and loss. The Advent journey strengthens our sincerity as we come to depend on God to continue giving us words of forgiveness and hope.

I invite you to enter into the silent voices of despair that you hear in the news, in your neighborhood, or in your family. In your quiet moments of prayer during this season, come to terms with your voice so you may use it to speak out about injustice, violence, and needless suffering. Become grateful for your prayerful silence because you have control over when you do not speak. Many people are forced into silence simply because no one gets close enough to listen. In your silent prayer, listen to the voice of the suffering.

1. God, my silent prayer is longing for

2. Jesus, open my heart to hear the voices of fear in

3. I long to be heard by God so that I

Action: Today, I will learn more about people living in poverty where I live.

Step 5. Prayer: Writing Your Way to New Birth

Take a minute or two to look back at what you have written. Then compose a short prayer offering whatever is in your heart to God. Write it in the space below or in the quiet of your heart and mind.

WEDNESDAY

Step 1. Welcome the Stranger Called Silence

Settle into your retreat space and sit in silence for a minute or two.

Step 2. Discover Your Story Within the Word

As you make the sign of the cross, pray:

O God, unshelter my heart that I may hear and know your holy Word.

Read the Sunday gospel passage in silence or aloud. Then spend another minute or two in silent reflection on the reading.

In what specific ways will you testify to the light of Christ's presence today?

Step 3. Connect to the Waiting World: Testify to the Light

Reflect on your action from yesterday.

How well have you met that goal?

Step 4. Respond to the Cry of the Prophets

John the Baptist also speaks for people whose voices we may never hear. During this Advent journey, I know I need to sit in silence and hear the voice of the newly widowed elderly woman who cries out because her children no longer speak with her. The nighttime cries of the Haitian orphaned child and the tears of the young trafficked girl in Thailand rise up in my Advent prayer. These loud cries and eternal tears I hear across nations, time, and place. These are also the ways in which I discover I belong to the world, to all societies, and to God's loving design.

Enter into the human voices that rage in the night. Even though you may never hear their physical voices, you may understand their experiences in your prayer. John the Baptist's strength of conviction gives us hope that we may also understand the voices that cry for real change, that rage against apathy and indifference, and that speak of a new way of loving in the world. Listen with all your present awareness to the invisible and silent voices of people suffering in our world.

How can you learn more about the voices of the world that need to be heard during this Advent season? How can you become a source of education for your parish or worshipping community on the need to become aware of these hidden voices? How can your need to belong be united to their need to be heard in the world? I encourage you to explore the options for continuing education about how to listen to the real voices of suffering that need to be healed.

1. When I listen in my silence in the face of a suffering world, I

2. God, open my heart to hear the voices of

3. Jesus, birth new hope in the cries of people who

Action: Today, I will study an issue of worldwide poverty.

Step 5. Prayer: Writing Your Way to New Birth

Take a minute or two to look back at what you have written. Then compose a short prayer offering whatever is in your heart to God. Write it in the space below or in the quiet of your heart and mind.

THURSDAY

Step 1. Welcome the Stranger Called Silence

Settle into your retreat space and sit in silence for a minute or two.

Step 2. Discover Your Story Within the Word

As you make the sign of the cross, pray:

O God, unshelter my heart that I may hear and know your holy Word.

Read the Sunday gospel passage in silence or aloud. Then spend another minute or two in silent reflection on the reading.

In what specific ways will you testify to the light of Christ's presence today?

Step 3. Connect to the Waiting World: Testify to the Light

Reflect on your action from yesterday.

How well have you met that goal?

Step 4. Respond to the Cry of the Prophets

The people who went into the desert to hear John the Baptist were also confused about his identity. "Who are you?" was the common question from people who were searching for new meaning and hope. This question may also be directed to our own lives: "Who am I?" We may be confused about our purpose and direction. We may feel stuck in our own destructive behaviors or our own lack of faith. Some people live with a sense that they never belong to anyone, even to themselves, let alone to God. This is an opportunity to change some of our old thinking about ourselves as we wait for the Messiah.

As our lives progress into the darkness of doubt, recurrent failure, or broken relationships, perhaps we need to think differently during Advent. Breaking out of our negative identities may not be easy for us. We may be used to seeing ourselves as not being good enough or worthy of much. In these Advent days, we need to listen to our voice, especially the negative aspects that constantly put others down (including ourselves).

How can you change your thinking about your own identity during Advent? Can you muster the courage to honestly ask the question, "Who am I?" Are you open to listening to your own negative voice? What are the negative attitudes that you need to change concerning how you live and the choices you have made? I invite you to ponder the mystery of your own life. Sit in silent prayer and listen to what God has to say about who you are.

1. Today, I hear my negative thoughts and comments, and I

2. God, allow me to recognize my identity in you so

3. Jesus, help me verbalize my need for

Action: Today, I will examine my relationships with my family and loved ones and see how negative thoughts have influenced how we treat one another.

Step 5. Prayer: Writing Your Way to New Birth

Take a minute or two to look back at what you have written. Then compose a short prayer offering whatever is in your heart to God. Write it in the space below or in the quiet of your heart and mind.

FRIDAY

Step 1. Welcome the Stranger Called Silence

Settle into your retreat space and sit in silence for a minute or two.

Step 2. Discover Your Story Within the Word

As you make the sign of the cross, pray:

O God, unshelter my heart that I may hear and know your holy Word.

Read the Sunday gospel passage in silence or aloud. Then spend another minute or two in silent reflection on the reading.

In what specific ways will you testify to the light of Christ's presence today?

Step 3. Connect to the Waiting World: Testify to the Light

Reflect on your action from yesterday.

How well have you met that goal?

Step 4. Respond to the Cry of the Prophets

John longed for people to enter fully into God's love and plan for them. He challenged people to make a straight path in their lives for the coming of God's kingdom. This path is a new relationship with mercy, grace, and love. The path that John spoke about was a path of the heart. He recognized the obstacles of sin, division, and pain and pointed us in the direction of God so healing could happen for every human heart. This is still God's plan for us.

God desires for all of us all that is good and loving. He waits for our hearts and minds to be open to such a gift. We may instinctively know that our harmful sin and our turning away from this love are the very places where we need to begin unsheltering our hearts. This Advent we may need to explore the ways in which we have deliberately turned from God's invitation of love and begin to straighten out our human desires, intentions, and life choices. We may fear this examination of our conscience because we do not want to be labeled sinners, or perhaps such a label already causes us to feel we do not belong in the Church or even in God's mercy. This examination of the human heart is not about finding a label of condemnation, but rather accepting an invitation for God to be born anew within our hearts.

How do you accept God's invitation to conversion and change? What in your heart longs for God's forgiveness and understanding?

How can you examine your actions and look forward to inviting God into your need? I encourage you to take stock of your life in this season of grace. God longs to be born within your yearning, to feel connected to every aspect of your humanity.

1. I need the mercy of God to heal my

2. God, welcome me on a straight path of love so I

3. God, forgive me so

Action: Today, I will examine my conscience in prayer.

Step 5. Prayer: Writing Your Way to New Birth

Take a minute or two to look back at what you have written. Then compose a short prayer offering whatever is in your heart to God. Write it in the space below or in the quiet of your heart and mind.

SATURDAY

Step 1. Welcome the Stranger Called Silence

Settle into your retreat space and sit in silence for a minute or two.

Step 2. Discover Your Story Within the Word

As you make the sign of the cross, pray:

O God, unshelter my heart that I may hear and know your holy Word.

Read the Sunday gospel passage in silence or aloud. Then spend another minute or two in silent reflection on the reading.

In what specific ways will you testify to the light of Christ's presence today?

Step 3. Connect to the Waiting World: Testify to the Light

Reflect on your action from yesterday.

How well have you met that goal?

Step 4. Respond to the Cry of the Prophets

John the Baptist's voice strengthened as he realized his life belonged in God. This humility led him into the desert to preach conversion and to baptize people who longed for a new life. His true passion was born in this humility. He claimed that Jesus would continue baptizing, but this time would baptize in the Holy Spirit. John told the people that he was an instrument of divine love and purpose, even though he felt unworthy to untie the sandals on Jesus' feet.

I know the fear-clenched heart does not rejoice. I am very conscious of my less-than-humble heart in these days of Advent. How can we turn our common fear into a new openness to divine grace and love? How can we wait for the dawn, released from fear and anxiety? How can we humbly approach the divine grace that longs to be born within our sheltered hearts? These questions ramble within my own shallowness during this Advent season. I ask you to bend your pride, raise your eyes to the dawn, and wait in joyful hope for the coming of Christ, the Savior.

1. I am anxious to welcome true joy because I must

2. Jesus, I offer my clenched heart to your mercy so

3. Jesus, in all humility I ask you

Action: Today, I will be grateful for every aspect of my life.

Step 5. Prayer: Writing Your Way to New Birth

Take a minute or two to look back at what you have written. Then compose a short prayer offering whatever is in your heart to God. Write it in the space below or in the quiet of your heart and mind.

Prayer for the Third Week of Advent

I hurriedly locked the outside doors of the chapel.
I had plans for dinner after Mass on the cold, rainy Saturday night.
A young man staggering on the sidewalk glared through the window.
He pounded on the glass and begged me to unlock the steel door.

Jesus, I let him enter the lobby and my life.
He grabbed my hands quickly and admitted his mental illness.
The twenty-something stranger sobbed in my arms.
The stranger whispered to me his name, "Albert."
He confessed he had been drinking and not taking his medication.

Albert fell to his knees and begged me to pray with him.
Jesus, he held my hands on his head so tightly.
He screamed for relief. He wanted to hear words of freedom.
Unplanned and unrehearsed words of prayer flew from my mouth.

I helped him to his feet, and he pushed open the door.
Tears streamed down his cheeks as he faced the cold.
Gratitude emerged from his soul: "I love you, Father."

Jesus, give us words to heal one another.
Give us a taste of our self-worth and receive our worry.
Help us become your voice of life and hope on cold nights.
Amen.

Do Not Be Afraid

SUNDAY

Step 1. Welcome the Stranger Called Silence

Settle into your retreat space and sit in silence for a minute or two.

Step 2. Discover Your Story Within the Word

As you make the sign of the cross, pray:

O God, unshelter my heart that I may hear and know your holy Word.

Read the Sunday gospel passage in silence or aloud.

Luke 1:26–38

The angel Gabriel was sent from God to a town of Galilee called Nazareth, to a virgin betrothed to a man named Joseph, of the house of David, and the virgin's name was Mary. And coming to her, he said, "Hail, full of grace! The Lord is with you." But she was greatly troubled at what was said and pondered what sort of greeting this might be. Then the angel said to her, "Do not be afraid, Mary, for you have found favor with God. Behold, you will conceive in your womb and

bear a son, and you shall name him Jesus. He will be great and will be called Son of the Most High, and the Lord God will give him the throne of David his father, and he will rule over the house of Jacob forever, and of his kingdom there will be no end." But Mary said to the angel, "How can this be, since I have no relations with a man?" And the angel said to her in reply, "The Holy Spirit will come upon you, and the power of the Most High will overshadow you. Therefore the child to be born will be called holy, the Son of God. And behold, Elizabeth, your relative, has also conceived a son in her old age, and this is the sixth month for her who was called barren; for nothing is impossible with God." Mary said, "Behold, I am the handmaid of the Lord. Let it be done to me according to your word." Then the angel departed from her.

Spend another minute or two in silent reflection on the reading.

Step 3. Connect to the Waiting World: Do Not Be Afraid

I long for the possibilities of God. I shudder as I hear the hushed words of a penitent woman express that the abuse she experienced as a child was her fault. Her ice-cold words linger in my heart as she says her adult life will never heal. I help an elderly man carry his backpack into the chapel, and he starts telling me that his cancer has returned, that he has come back to Portland to die on the streets. I start to cross the street outside our chapel, and I see a twenty-something youth so stoned that his body is freezing. He is in the middle of the street, in the tracks of the city train.

I am so afraid for people's survival. Even though we are all afraid, these encounters stir in me a deeper respect for each person on earth. As I enter into these relationships, I see more clearly a sincere moment of faith. I open my eyes to what is real, and there emerges in my awkward heart a new belief that God is still here. Even in these bleak circumstances, each human life carries the possibility and wonder of God's love.

I am humbled to the earth by how people carry on in adulthood in the face of unimaginable family neglect. I am speechless as people share their secrets of mental anguish, job loss, long-term diseases, and daily hunger. In these uncertain moments, I feel my own powerlessness to affirm people, because I cannot cure, fix, or heal anyone. I believe this is the place we receive the message either from one angel or another not to become afraid in this life. I must believe with my entire being that people are cared for, that every life has meaning, and that we will all be consoled by God's presence.

In these fragile relationships, I experience what is possible in God. I cannot imagine how Mary felt when this winged heavenly power approached her to do something unimaginable. I am sure she was humbled when a voice from beyond said that she would be part of a plan to invite grace, comfort, and healing into the world. I believe these events are still happening. Not that any one of us will stand before a bright light or hear a consoling voice from the unknown, but our being an instrument of healing is still in God's plan.

I am sure Mary's word and conviction must have changed even the cynic's mind about what God can do on earth. I admit I am still trying with all my might to convince some people that others need a helping hand or a healing presence. I invite people visiting from local expensive hotels to worship with us, and some people will not even enter the building because the stench from our guests lingers long after the hospitality hours have ended. I give talks, write articles, and send letters; but still some people blame those who are sick for being sick or people who have no jobs for being unemployed. I wait with Mary to hear, and not to be afraid, when people need consolation and new life.

In this fourth Sunday of Advent, the clanging voices of the ancient prophets are replaced with a subtle example of fearlessness. The ranting and raving of John, pointing with all his might into the direction of God, are being replaced with the quiet acquiescence of a young girl who is preparing to change the world. The sacred liturgy that rouses us from sleep to wake our very souls to work for justice and a new order is now tender, quiet, with genuine hope. I stand with those prophets shaking my fists for change, and I also kneel with my hands open in genuine humility that God has a plan.

I come to this fourth Sunday of Advent in great awe because I cannot chart or diagram any revelation of God's care for us. Like Mary and so many other believers before me, I must trust beyond my imagination. I willingly offer every aspect of my sheltered heart to God, who expects to pry open my stubbornness. Mary's subtle openness in her youth shows me in my adulthood how to wait for everything for others and for myself.

Luke puts into the mouths and lives of people who have no worldly power the realization of God's involvement with everyone. This is the true Advent message. Mary, the ordinary young person wanting to experience love, instead lives a message from an angel that will rattle kings and conquerors. Her prophetic posture of openness shows us even in our day how to stand up for people who live in fear, dread, and worry. Mary received the angel as her heart became unsheltered, open, and transparent for God's arrival.

Luke's choice of putting into the mouth of the powerless the real strength of God teaches us to do the same. From the prophetic words of the people surviving poverty I receive a greater experience of trust and love. I learn that my attachments to wealth, education, power, and even priestly authority are not ends to love but only a means to understand a greater dependence on God. People overcoming severe hardships strengthen my life of genuine prayer, real integrity, and personal honesty. I depend on the gritty candor of the marginalized to humble me and offer me a genuine sense of belonging and purpose in Christ Jesus.

I do not have the personal strength to change people's lives, opinions, or faith. However, I am being called to find room in my sheltered heart to receive the message from God that is more powerful than what I could ever dream. I am called first to believe that the Incarnation—God's presence in the world—is also for *my* life. I belong to God. This is the message not only from an angel but also from Mary's response. As I minister among the marginalized, I will never give a word of hope to others without first receiving this message from within. I will never become an example of love without first being open to God, who heals my experiences, my memories, and lasting wounds and calls me into the thick of being an adult believer.

Step 4. Respond to the Cry of the Prophets

Mary, the young prophet, demonstrates to all people the possibilities of God. She anticipated a future as a wife. Her dreams and plans fit in with her tradition and family history. However, God invited her to reorder her life, to change her plans, and to trust in him. Mary's expectations for her own life could never have measured up to what God wanted of her.

On this last Sunday of Advent, we hear within our own lives the subtle sounds of prophets. We place ourselves among angel voices, in the mix of splendid dreaming and the overwhelming care of God. Mary models for us a rich relationship in God. We are not excluded from those ancient dreams or heavenly voices. The reality of Christ's passion, death, and resurrection invites every follower into the deep mystery of grace. Every person finds a place in God, a home in the sacred voice of love.

We prepare for the celebration of Christ's birth. However, we do not look for grace hidden in the past or completed among the scriptural prophets. Unless we celebrate Jesus now in our day, grace is lost and forever trapped in an ancient generation. God is alive today, calling us all to complete love. This love is for every human person. No person is excluded, condemned, or withdrawn from this perfect love. In this busy season, how do we center our lives on the continuing compassion of God? How do we rest in the perfect presence of Christ already in our midst? These are the genuine invitations of God in this holy season.

1. I must shed my reluctance to be loved by God and

2. Mary shows me that my instinct to dream is

3. I have missed the love Jesus has for me because of my attitudes of

Action: Today, I will be grateful for my imperfections.

Step 5. Prayer: Writing Your Way to New Birth

Take a minute or two to look back at what you have written. Then compose a short prayer offering whatever is in your heart to God. Write it in the space below or in the quiet of your heart and mind.

MONDAY

Step 1. Welcome the Stranger Called Silence

Settle into your retreat space and sit in silence for a minute or two.

Step 2. Discover Your Story Within the Word

As you make the sign of the cross, pray:

O God, unshelter my heart that I may hear and know your holy Word.

Read the Sunday gospel passage (pp. 63–64) in silence or aloud. Then spend another minute or two in silent reflection on the reading.

What fear will you face and begin to release today?

Step 3. Connect to the Waiting World: Do Not Be Afraid

You may wish to revisit the thematic essay on pages 64–66 if it will help you focus your retreat time.

Take a couple of minutes to think about how well you did with your action from yesterday. Journal about it if that is useful.

Step 4. Respond to the Cry of the Prophets

Mary honestly expressed her fear. She was troubled and afraid at the sight of Gabriel. However, even in her very human response, she faced the miraculous. In these closing days of Advent, we come to welcome genuine honesty within our lives. We open our hearts to divine voices, yet our feet are planted firmly on the ground. We listen to messages sent to Mary telling her not to be afraid; but we still know the terror of bodily pain, broken promises, and unstable lives. God does not take away our fear, but God remains at the center and core of our existence.

Our honest fear is the place where love is born. This is the real treasure we find this week if we are willing to open our lives to this celebration of the Incarnation. As we center on the child Jesus this week, we know our adult fear will be the window to new life and courage. Believe that you are also called into God's love and presence. Believe in the last days of Advent that God rests in your heart, amid your insecurity.

How can you work through any fear that shrouds your life? How do you recognize new life when you see it? Are you too used to living with cynicism, hatred, and inner violence? Continue your journey inward, going deeper into the mystery of God's plan among us. Orient the darkness that surrounds your heart into the direction of the angel's voice of compassion. Hear for yourself that fear is useless and that within real trust lies the power of love, fidelity, and God's divine care.

1. I continue to hold fear in my life because

2. I find it so difficult to trust God because

3. As the days get closer to Christmas, I feel

Action: Today, I will talk to someone about my fear.

Step 5. Prayer: Writing Your Way to New Birth

Take a minute or two to look back at what you have written. Then compose a short prayer offering whatever is in your heart to God. Write it in the space below or in the quiet of your heart and mind.

TUESDAY

Step 1. Welcome the Stranger Called Silence

Settle into your retreat space and sit in silence for a minute or two.

Step 2. Discover Your Story Within the Word

As you make the sign of the cross, pray:

O God, unshelter my heart that I may hear and know your holy Word.

Read the Sunday gospel passage in silence or aloud. Then spend another minute or two in silent reflection on the reading.

What fear will you face and begin to release today?

Step 3. Connect to the Waiting World: Do Not Be Afraid

Reflect on your action from yesterday.

How well have you met that goal?

Step 4. Respond to the Cry of the Prophets

The angel Gabriel revealed God's plan to Mary. Mary began with profound questions. She wondered what sort of greeting this might be and how she could be with child. In this profound human exchange with a divine voice, we receive a model of love and fidelity in the face of human logic and earthly possibility. We also may be at a similar point of profound questioning. We may be at a loss as to how this season of Advent will prove beneficial in our own lives. At the same time, we may be at an essential moment of transformation, looking up to heaven and wondering what our future will entail.

I invite you into this powerful, contemplative moment in the scriptures and in the life of Mary. Center your reflection today on this moment of Mary's questioning. Do not be afraid to raise your mind, heart, and prayer toward heaven and sincerely question your future. Enter deeply into this unknown moment, this uncertain place; experience this powerless presence with God and try to trust. This is a place of discovering God in our human circumstances and our questions about our future.

God hears our questions born of uncertainty and pain. All of our futures on earth are unknown, but we are all called to live our lives in faith. We may be called to demonstrate the divine presence within us, a presence that seems hidden. We may be asked to offer the world our talents that seem slim or even worthless. We may be called to step out of the darkness of our self-preoccupation and be a model of love for the world. What does it feel like to enter into this moment of uncertainty? Can you truly live even for a moment in this exchange of silent powerlessness and trust? Can you accept that this silent questioning about your life is a holy place, a divine moment?

1. Today, my questions about my future seem so

2. I desire to entrust my future into God's plan, but I

3. Open my heart today, God, and allow me

Action: Today, I will trust God's plan for my life.

Step 5. Prayer: Writing Your Way to New Birth

Take a minute or two to look back at what you have written. Then compose a short prayer offering whatever is in your heart to God. Write it in the space below or in the quiet of your heart and mind.

WEDNESDAY

Step 1. Welcome the Stranger Called Silence

Settle into your retreat space and sit in silence for a minute or two.

Step 2. Discover Your Story Within the Word

As you make the sign of the cross, pray:

O God, unshelter my heart that I may hear and know your holy Word.

Read the Sunday gospel passage in silence or aloud. Then spend another minute or two in silent reflection on the reading.

What fear will you face and begin to release today?

Step 3. Connect to the Waiting World: Do Not Be Afraid

Reflect on your action from yesterday.

How well have you met that goal?

Step 4. Respond to the Cry of the Prophets

"Do not be afraid, Mary." These words spoken by Gabriel, a divine being, echo God's desire for new life, inner peace, and the Incarnation. These words become a spiritual pathway for the divine plan. We hear these words when there is a new presence of Christ in the world. We hear these holy words in our human worry when we are about to encounter Christ in a new way. We hear them at the Annunciation and at the birth of Christ. We enter into these words of consolation at Christ's resurrection and at the moment of Pentecost. These words reminding us not to be afraid are keys in the story of Jesus that open a new awareness within all believers, indicating that grace is taking place.

People are afraid when they face twists and turns in their lives and endure unfortunate consequences of their actions. For some people fear is long-term, lasting through years of mental illness, crippling disease, and catastrophic loss. No matter why we are afraid, we are called again in these last days of Advent to hear from a divine source that fear need not endure. Fear becomes the birthplace of God, a new way of being in the world for everyone. Fear gives birth to Jesus, so we may all believe that God cares for us.

Open your imagination to Gabriel's words of fearlessness. Take seriously these moments in the scriptural story. Hear with your own heart, with all of your uncertainty and pain of the past, a message of freedom. We can hear these words only if we first live in moments of prayer and silence. In this frantic week of Christmas preparation, we may be unable to hear these words. However, this is the one week of the year that we most need to hear them. This is also the week of the year that profound loneliness, anger among family members, and disappointments with our own lives come to be born in our minds, hearts, and actions. What will it take for you to settle into the message of Gabriel?

1. Today, I am afraid because I still

2. I so desire to offer my family

3. I realize my fear says that I

Action: Today, I will examine my lifetime regrets and not be afraid of tomorrow.

Step 5. Prayer: Writing Your Way to New Birth

Take a minute or two to look back at what you have written. Then compose a short prayer offering whatever is in your heart to God. Write it in the space below or in the quiet of your heart and mind.

THURSDAY

Step 1. Welcome the Stranger Called Silence

Settle into your retreat space and sit in silence for a minute or two.

Step 2. Discover Your Story Within the Word

As you make the sign of the cross, pray:

O God, unshelter my heart that I may hear and know your holy Word.

Read the Sunday gospel passage in silence or aloud. Then spend another minute or two in silent reflection on the reading.

What fear will you face and begin to release today?

Step 3. Connect to the Waiting World: Do Not Be Afraid

Reflect on your action from yesterday.

How well have you met that goal?

Step 4. Respond to the Cry of the Prophets

Mary has found favor with God. This message from the angel Gabriel is at the root of our existence on earth. God has redeemed us through Jesus' passion, death, and resurrection. Gabriel's message to Mary foretells the resurrection of the life she carries within her. Mary offers us the favor of God through her own life. The favor of God means that we are all loved and forgiven in Christ Jesus. We all belong in this miracle of life, this treasure of grace on earth. Nothing will keep us from this favor now. Christ's life has accomplished everything for us sinners and doubters, for us who think we live on the margins of love in the world.

So many people have been told their entire lives that their very existence does not matter in the world. People have been locked in this horrific notion of life because of sexual abuse, bullying, or the effects of long-term poverty. Many people are put down and shunned and have their spirits squelched because of not feeling loved by any person on earth. No wonder experiencing divine love is so complicated for so many people. God seems so inaccessible and difficult to trust.

I invite you to sit with this message from Gabriel. Pray the words of the angel silently within your heart. Pray these words out loud from your own lips. Listen to yourself say the words of Gabriel, "You have found favor with God." Ponder the presence of the angel within your own life, and greet these words with a new fidelity and purpose. Be strong and courageous and believe deeply that God's faithfulness is for you, coming to you from the divine voice of Gabriel. How can you listen with your entire being to these words of Gabriel? What do you have to lose to truly listen to them? How can you receive such a revelation of love this week?

1. Jesus, help me live your message of love for me so that

2. I long to hear God's message of

3. Jesus, be born in my heart so I

Action: Today, I will create a plan to serve people in need this coming year.

Step 5. Prayer: Writing Your Way to New Birth

Take a minute or two to look back at what you have written. Then compose a short prayer offering whatever is in your heart to God. Write it in the space below or in the quiet of your heart and mind.

FRIDAY

Step 1. Welcome the Stranger Called Silence

Settle into your retreat space and sit in silence for a minute or two.

Step 2. Discover Your Story Within the Word

As you make the sign of the cross, pray:

O God, unshelter my heart that I may hear and know your holy Word.

Read the Sunday gospel passage in silence or aloud. Then spend another minute or two in silent reflection on the reading.

What fear will you face and begin to release today?

Step 3. Connect to the Waiting World: Do Not Be Afraid

Reflect on your action from yesterday.

How well have you met that goal?

Step 4. Respond to the Cry of the Prophets

The angel's message reassured Mary that the Holy Spirit was present within her. This gift of God must have seemed just as strange as the angel to a young girl confused about her place in God. In our lives, the Holy Spirit's work may often seem just as strange and contrary to our humanity. We live in the depths of this relationship with God through the gift of faith in our own baptism. For Mary, the encounter with this angel seems to be a baptism in the richness of God's love for her, even in her confusion and doubt.

As we proceed to the celebration of the Incarnation, of God becoming flesh for our salvation, we also recognize again the gifts of the Holy Spirit among us. This Spirit of God calls us all ever deeper into the mystery of God, into the life that even seems contrary to our own instincts and plans. The Spirit of God invites us to reflect on our own relationship with God, especially in the unexpected and confusing moments of our lives.

I ask you to examine again where you have witnessed God's action in your life. Pray through some of the scenes in your life that led you to a new openness, a selfless giving, or a healing discovery as to how to view life's situations. When were you confused about life and then something happened to open you to new possibilities in God? What were the conflicts, decisions, and turning points that led to that encounter with God? What were the moments of surprise in your life when you knew in your heart that God was near? How did you respond to the workings of the Holy Spirit, the guidance of God that seemed certain and true?

1. I need so desperately to rely on God at this time so that

2. If I can settle into the gift of the Holy Spirit in my life, I usually feel

3. God, grant the gift of your healing Spirit so that

Action: Today, I will be a messenger of reconciliation to someone in need.

Step 5. Prayer: Writing Your Way to New Birth

Take a minute or two to look back at what you have written. Then compose a short prayer offering whatever is in your heart to God. Write it in the space below or in the quiet of your heart and mind.

SATURDAY

Step 1. Welcome the Stranger Called Silence

Settle into your retreat space and sit in silence for a minute or two.

Step 2. Discover Your Story Within the Word

As you make the sign of the cross, pray:

O God, unshelter my heart that I may hear and know your holy Word.

Read the Sunday gospel passage in silence or aloud. Then spend another minute or two in silent reflection on the reading.

What fear will you face and begin to release today?

Step 3. Connect to the Waiting World: Do Not Be Afraid

Reflect on your action from yesterday.

How well have you met that goal?

Step 4. Respond to the Cry of the Prophets

Mary discovered that even her family relationships were being touched with the gift of the Holy Spirit. Her cousin, Elizabeth, was also with child. Elizabeth's son was to be the forerunner of Jesus. Her expectations of life, her plans, and her future were being guided by the gift of God's presence. This was truly miraculous, unexpected and grace-filled. Mary's acceptance of this gift gives us all courage to be with our families during this season of grace.

During this season of Advent, stress and fear often mount among our relationships and can weaken family ties. Sometimes we make judgments about our relatives' lives without really understanding them. We can put them down, judging them by our standards. We forget that the Holy Spirit is also guiding them, and they are living their lives as they have come to understand them.

As Advent ends, I invite you into the prayer of the Holy Spirit for the healing of your own life. I also encourage you to pray in the Holy Spirit that God grant you a new sense of relationship with relatives, friends, and colleagues—the relationships that have been torn or fractured. How can you learn to trust the Holy Spirit in your own life? What are the areas of burden, apathy, and denial in which you need to feel the healing presence of God? As Advent ends, rest in the healing grace and love of the Holy Spirit.

1. As I face my relatives and friends this season, God is being born in me so that

2. My unexpected and grace-filled moments with friends this Advent teach me

3. God, I realize now in a deeper way that I belong in your love, so offer me now

Action: Today, I will express my joy for God's love in our world.

Step 5. Prayer: Writing Your Way to New Birth

Take a minute or two to look back at what you have written. Then compose a short prayer offering whatever is in your heart to God. Write it in the space below or in the quiet of your heart and mind.

Prayer for the Fourth Week of Advent

I arrived at the hospital room with great reluctance.
I was asked to anoint a man dying of cancer.
His two young, beautiful daughters greeted me at the door.
A cherub-faced grandson bounced on his mother's hip.
The articulate sisters told me stories of their father's fidelity.

The man's elderly mother held my hand tightly and rested in my eyes.
She told me details of her son's tragedies and illnesses.
I was enveloped in generational warmth and care.

Jesus, we all stood around his bed to pray.
He was unable to speak, and they cried tears of prayer.
One daughter clung to the happy baby. One daughter held her father.
His mother wept her loss and assured him of her love.

Jesus, my heart landed on the baby grinning in the midst of tears.
The mother held him tenderly as if she were holding the world's future.
I listened to these holy women and watched the new child.
Jesus, I witnessed the old dying and the new being born.

Amen.

Ronald Patrick Raab, C.S.C., ministers among the vulnerable and marginalized of society and the Church. From his experiences in living the Gospel among the poor, he speaks and writes about prayer and service and knowing the love of God through our common poverty. He hosts *On the Margins*, a weekly radio scripture commentary on KBVM 88.3 FM, Catholic Broadcasting Northwest. He is active as a retreat director, workshop presenter, blogger, and award-winning author. He contributes regularly to several liturgy magazines, including *Ministry & Liturgy* and *Celebrate!* Raab serves as associate pastor at the Downtown Chapel in Portland, Oregon. Visit him online at ronaldraab.blogspot.com.

Founded in 1865, Ave Maria Press, a ministry of the Congregation of Holy Cross, is a Catholic publishing company that serves the spiritual and formative needs of the Church and its schools, institutions, and ministers; Christian individuals and families; and others seeking spiritual nourishment.

For a complete listing of titles from

Ave Maria Press

Sorin Books

Forest of Peace

Christian Classics

visit www.avemariapress.com

ave maria press® / Notre Dame, IN 46556
A Ministry of the United States Province of Holy Cross